S0-BFA-010

RLICBARBECUEDCAJUNBUFFALO

WING IT!

Delectable recipes for
everyone's favorite bar snack

WING IT!

CHRISTOPHER B. O'HARA

PHOTOGRAPHS BY WILLIAM A. NASH

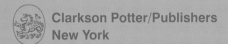
Clarkson Potter/Publishers
New York

Copyright © 2004 by Christopher B. O'Hara

All rights reserved. No part of this book may be reproduced or transmitted in any form or by any means, electronic or mechanical, including photocopying, recording, or by any information storage and retrieval system, without permission in writing from the publisher.

Published by Clarkson Potter/Publishers, New York, New York.
Member of the Crown Publishing Group, a division of Random House, Inc.
www.crownpublishing.com

CLARKSON N. POTTER is a trademark and POTTER and colophon are registered trademarks of Random House, Inc.

Printed in Singapore

Design by Jane Treuhaft

Library of Congress Cataloging-in-Publication Data
O'Hara, Christopher B.
        Wing it! / Christopher B. O'Hara
Includes index.
1. Cookery (Chicken).   I. Title.
        TX750.5.C45057   2003
        641.6'65—dc22   2003015010

ISBN 1-4000-5117-7

10   9   8   7   6   5   4   3   2   1

First Edition

TO HOLLAND O'HARA,
MY NEW BEST FRIEND

CONTENTS

In 1964, the lowly chicken wing—widely considered at that time to be the gastronomical equivalent to the pig's knuckle—stepped out of America's soup pots and into the limelight when one Mrs. Teressa Bellissimo of Buffalo, New York, deep-fried a batch of chicken wings for her son and his friends and served them with blue cheese dressing. That single act of culinary improvisation had far-reaching effects—thirty-eight years later, chicken wings have become a part of the appetizer vernacular, and not just in the local sports pub. Since Americans enjoy an average of eighty-two pounds of chicken per person every year, a wide range of tasty wing recipes has arisen, which offers a nearly endless number of ways to enjoy this classic snack.

The wing has come a long way from its Tabasco-soaked origins in Buffalo's Anchor Bar. There is an endless variety of ways to eat America's favorite football snack—from Southern style to Korean flavored and everything in between. One of the most versatile foods, wings can be baked, barbecued, smoked, or deep-fried—and can be served with a host of complementary sauces ranging from the typical (blue cheese salad dressing) to the unusual (Beaujolais currant glaze with orange zest). There are, literally, endless possibilities.

The scope of this book, however, is limited to fun, easy recipes that make the perfect finger food. You won't need to be a seasoned chef to make any of the recipes, and you can be sure that your party guests will appreciate having something different to munch, not the same old tired chips and salsa, cheese and crackers, or pigs-in-a-blanket. Everybody loves wings, and I hope that this little book helps you enjoy preparing them even more.

A BRIEF HISTORY OF WINGS

Even though chickens were domesticated more than eight thousand years ago (and were a popular menu item long before that), the chicken wing never captured the popular imagination in the same way as chicken Kiev or chicken pot pie. Most of the time, chicken wings were added to gizzards and necks and used to flavor chicken stock or they were merely discarded. Although the advent of refrigeration and the commercialization of the poultry market soon offered consumers a dizzying array of prepackaged chicken parts, the chicken wing was more of a staple food for primarily poorer families, since the ratio of meat to skin is very low. It would be a long time before chicken wings were prepackaged separately—and, ultimately, became an industry unto themselves.

With Americans consuming more than eight billion chickens per year (you do the wing math), it was lucky that Buffalo's Teressa Bellissimo had unknowingly created culinary history. Despite some controversy surrounding its ori-

gins, most poultry scholars agree that the first order of Buffalo wings was created in her kitchen at the Anchor Bar when she was inspired to offload a heaping mound of soup-pot–bound chicken wings into the deep-fryer, drain them, cover them with margarine and spicy chile pepper sauce, and serve them with a heaping helping of "bleu" cheese dressing. That single act of frenzied improvisation created gastronomic ripples still felt to this day. In Buffalo, July 29 is officially "Chicken Wing Day." In 2001, Buffalo's first annual National Buffalo Wing Festival drew more than 45,000 people who consumed nearly 20 tons of chicken wings.

The spicy, deep-fried wing didn't stay confined to the relatively bucolic area of Buffalo for long. With prices for a pound of wings in the pennies (about a nickel in 1964) and customers eager to shell out dollars for a heaping plate of the spicy appetizer, a new bar and restaurant profit center was born. Spicy wings also helped plump bar receipts significantly as consumers washed down cold beer to quench the thirst brought on by salty sodium-laden blue cheese dressing and the fiery bite of Tabasco sauce. Within years, wings were a ubiquitous menu offering from coast to coast.

CHICKEN WINGS

The first thing you need to have in order to prepare chicken wings is, well, chicken. Most supermarkets have prepackaged wings in large quantities—some of them already disjointed and ready to cook. The larger, meatier, and fresher the wing, the better. Many large supermarket chains and wholesale stores offer large portions of Grade A wings in frozen packages, which is perfectly fine. Always remember to thoroughly wash the wings in cold water, and allow them to drain under refrigeration before cooking. I usually place the washed wings on a covered baking sheet in the refrigerator for several hours, and let the water and excess blood completely drain from the wings prior to cooking them. This method results in a much crispier wing—especially if you are deep-frying them.

To ensure you are purchasing the freshest chicken, be sure to follow these basic precepts of food safety when preparing chicken:

- **Always make chicken the last thing you buy before you leave the supermarket.**
- **Pick chicken from the bottom of the meat case, where temperatures are coolest. Make sure the packaging is sealed tightly.**
- **Immediately place chicken in a produce bag, to prevent leakage, which can infect other food in a grocery cart.**
- **Do not refrigerate chicken for more than two days—if you aren't planning on eating it immediately, freeze it.**
- **Wash hands that come into contact with raw chicken before preparing other foods, and always disinfect surfaces that have been in contact with raw chicken.**
- **Discard chicken marinades after use. If you are using a marinade to baste chicken on the grill during cooking, make sure the chicken cooks at a high temperature for several minutes after applying the marinade in order to kill off any germs.**

BLUE CHEESE

I think one of the things that makes our obsession with Buffalo wings so intense is the unlikely yet wonderful marriage of fried chicken and blue cheese dressing. Although there are many delicious store-bought dressings available that go perfectly well with wings, it is fun to experiment on your own with creating different types of blue cheese dressing. Plus, the flavor of fresh blue cheese cannot be found in a bottled dressing.

So, what exactly is blue (or "bleu") cheese? Basically, it's cheese that has been injected with mold spores (*Penicillium roqueforti,* to be precise) that, when mixed with air, produce natural enzymes that break down the cheese to give it an incredible flavor and texture. There are several different types of blue cheese, all with a distinctive flavor and texture resulting from the source of milk and the preparation method specific to each. Some favorites to look for are Gorgonzola, the buttery Italian blue cheese from Lombardy; Roquefort, the French blue made from sheep's milk and aged in caves; Maytag, the American blue created at Iowa's Maytag Dairy Farm in 1941; and Stilton, the famous English blue cheese made from summer cow milk.

HOT PEPPER SAUCES

Many of the wing recipes in this book—and the Buffalo wing recipes in particular—call for a liberal application of hot sauce. Over the past several years, there has been incredible growth in the number and variety of hot sauces available. Whereas in the past you were limited to Tabasco or RedHot, the hot sauce connoisseur can now choose from hundreds of different specialty sauces ranging from mild to "insanity"-type heat levels. For hot wings, the trick is to give a satisfying kick without destroying the flavor of the chicken and other spices. The original Anchor Bar recipe for Buffalo wings calls for Frank's RedHot sauce, which is quite mild. The key to cooking with hot pepper sauces is knowing that you can always add more—so start with less and adjust the recipe to your particular taste.

SOME POPULAR HOT SAUCE BRANDS

Frank's RedHot Cayenne Pepper Sauce is the "original" hot sauce used for Buffalo wings, and a fine one to boot. Although dwarfed in popularity by the better-known Tabasco sauce, RedHot truly lives up to its credo of providing "the perfect blend of flavor and heat." Frank's introduces the delicious flavor and zing of chile peppers without overwhelming the palate.

Tabasco is the undisputed king of pepper sauces. Claiming a Scoville rating of only 2,500 to 5,000 units, it barely comes close to any of the more incendiary sauces available on the market—but it's plenty hot enough. A bit hotter than Frank's, Tabasco has a unique flavor and tang that go hand-in-hand with spicy wings. Tabasco has recently introduced a green pepper sauce made from milder jalapeño peppers, a super-hot habanero pepper sauce, and a dark and smoky chipotle sauce—all worth trying.

Cholula is another popular sauce, made by the folks who distill Jose Cuervo tequila. Easily recognizable by its bottle's wooden top, this excellent sauce is made from a blend of red and piquin peppers in Jalisco, Mexico. This has more flavor than bite, and is exceptionally good in wing sauces, dips, and marinades.

Of course, there are literally thousands of super-hot chile pepper sauces, most of which are marketed as "the hottest." These brands are often charac-terized by hyperbolic names evocative of either their ability to cause gastrointestinal distress (i.e., Ass Blaster, Ass in Space, et al.); the mental health of the consumer (Insanity, Total Insanity, etc.); or the danger involved in consuming the sauce itself (Death Sauce, Widow: No Survivors, and so on). Although there are some generally good sauces out there to pick from, I generally advise against these sauces as they are quite dangerously hot and tend to kill off other flavors in your food. If you simply can't stay away, go to www.peppers.com and take your pick.

COOKING METHODS

Chicken wings, just like every other part of this amazingly versatile fowl, can be cooked to perfection in innumerable ways. From baking and grilling to broiling and frying, each method has its distinct advantages depending on the recipe. Since cooking the wings themselves is a fairly simple process, I offer you this simple wing-cooking guide, broken down by cooking method. Throughout the book, I will often ask you to "cook the wings according to the method described on page 19," and ask that you refer to the instructions herein.

The first thing to know about chicken wings is their three distinct parts: the large wing joint, or "drumette," which looks like a mini-drumstick; the middle joint, which is the meaty part of the wing; and the small wing joint, which is the very tip of the wing, which is basically nothing but skin and bone. Use a good, sharp pair of poultry shears to separate the joints, so as not to disturb the skin. If you are of an economical mind, you can save the wing tips for chicken stock. Or, you can just keep them on. As a secret pork rind lover, I personally like the way they come out of the deep-fryer or barbecue—all burnt and crispy. Where recipes call for the "small wing joint removed," you can leave the rest of the wing whole, or separate the two remaining joints.

FRYING METHODS

Chicken wings are certainly one of life's guilty pleasures—a food that must be consumed without regard to its impact on one's diet. Many of the chicken wing recipes call for deep-frying, and for good reason: It is the traditional and preferred method of preparing wings. It is also very easy, once you learn a few practical tips and techniques. There are two types of deep-frying: pan-frying and deep-fat frying. In the former, oil is heated in a deep pan and the food is cooked on the stovetop. In the latter, an appliance is used to heat the oil and keep it at a set temperature, and the food is lowered into the oil by means of a mesh basket. Regardless of which method you choose, the oil you use has

a big effect on the success of your wings. I recommend peanut oil since it adds flavor, is more resistant to splatter than vegetable oils, and has a high smoking point. It also holds up better than vegetable oil, taking longer to discolor and spoil. If you don't have peanut oil, vegetable oil is fine—it is also less expensive.

DEEP-FAT FRYING

If you plan on doing more than just occasional frying, you should purchase a deep-fat fryer. Decent models can be had for a very reasonable price and, even if you think you have little use for one, you will find yourself using it more and more once you do. Deep-fat fryers hold more food, eliminate splatter during cooking, keep the oil at a steady temperature without burning it, and mitigate the very real concern of kitchen fires. They are very simple to operate, easy to clean, and economical, as the cooking oil is kept cleaner, enabling multiple uses. The keys to successful deep-fat frying are simple: Always batter your wings, keep your oil hot enough, and don't crowd the basket with food. Battering the wings before frying (even if it's just with a light dusting of flour) provides a protective barrier for the wings, ensuring they don't absorb unhealthy amounts of oil. Another key is to keep your oil at the proper temperature. Too hot, and your oil will reach the smoking point; not hot enough, and your food will absorb oil and come out greasy. Always cook wings at a minimum of 175 degrees Fahrenheit to ensure the best results. Most deep-fat fryers have a temperature gauge. If not, a deep-fryer thermometer is a great asset. If you don't have a thermometer, test the temperature by dropping in a small piece of bread or potato. If it browns within 45 seconds to a minute, you are on track.

Method for Deep-frying Wings in a Fryer Heat the peanut or vegetable oil to a temperature of 175 degrees. Carefully place the wings into the hot oil in batches, being careful not to overcrowd the frying basket. I recommend cooking twelve to fifteen wings at a time, depending on the size. Cook for 12 to 15 minutes, until the wings are medium-crispy outside. Drain the wings on a large baking sheet covered with paper towels or the unprinted side of grocery bags. To be safe, test the wings with a meat thermometer to make sure they have a minimum interior temperature of 170 degrees Fahrenheit.

PAN-FRYING

If you don't have a deep-fat fryer, you will need to fry your wings in a large, deep frying pan or wok. The cooking principles are the same as in deep-fat frying, but you'll need to be more hands-on when frying your wings the old-fashioned way. That means monitoring the temperature and keeping your wings cooking evenly in the oil. To cook fifteen wings at a time, you will need between 2 and 4 cups of oil—enough to fully immerse them. You will want a pan that's large enough to accommodate this number of wings without crowding. You can reduce splatter—and the potential for an oil fire—by leaving approximately 3 inches of space between the oil and the top of the pan.

Method for Pan-frying Wings To pan-fry your wings, fill your frying pan halfway with oil and, over a high flame, heat it to 375 degrees. Be careful not to let the flames reach over the side of the pan. Once the oil reaches 375, lower the heat and maintain a steady temperature. Remove excess batter from the wings, and gently slide them into the pan, or lower them into the pan using a slotted spoon. Cook for 12 to 15 minutes, until the wings achieve a medium-crispy exterior texture. Drain the wings on a large baking sheet covered with paper towels or the unprinted side of grocery bags.

DEEP-FRYING TIPS

If your wings must wait before being served, place the wings on a large baking sheet and put them in the oven with the door slightly ajar to allow circulation. Covering the wings will make them soggy.

Replace the oil frequently. When the oil begins to darken, it should be replaced. Darkening is a sign that the oil is breaking down, which causes smoking and can impart a bad flavor. Excessive foaming around cooking food, oil that's smoking at normal cooking temperatures, and a rancid smell are all signs that your cooking oil should be replaced immediately.

Fry safely. Never leave your fryer unattended while cooking. Dry your wings before putting them into the fryer to avoid excessive splatter. And be sure to choose a fryer with a thermostat control to prevent overheating.

Storing and Preserving Oil Your deep-frying oil can be reused about three times, if you follow these guidelines. Try not to preheat oil for long periods, as the longer that oil is heated, the more quickly it will break down and discolor. Always shake off excess flour or batter from your wings before putting them into the fryer, to avoid small particles that burn easily and cloud the oil. Use cheesecloth or coffee filters to strain cold oil into your storage container, and remember to store in a cool place or the refrigerator to maintain freshness.

GRILLING/BARBECUING

Chicken and the grill go hand-in-hand, and chicken wings made on the grill are especially easy to prepare—and mess-free. What's better than serving a special treat of wings to your barbecue guests before the main course? After all, the grill's already going. . . . The best way to cook chicken on the grill is to barbecue it. Although we often use the words *grill* and *barbecue* interchangeably, they are two very different cooking methods.

Grilling is the act of placing food directly over a flame. Barbecuing, on the other hand, is the method of cooking slowly through indirect heat. You can grill wings, but they are much better barbecued.

Method for Barbecuing Wings on the Grill The key to achieving moist and tender wings is even, steady, indirect heat. Heat your barbecue to a minimum of 350 degrees (low to medium heat) and prepare the coals so they are hot and even burning, with a coating of white ash on top. Spread your coals along the outer perimeter of the grill, so that the actual cooking surface you place your wings on will not be in direct contact with open flames. Place the wings on the grill, away from open flame. Barbecue, lid down, for 25 to 30 minutes, or until the wings have a crispy, browned appearance. If you are using a marinade, baste wings frequently throughout cooking and sear them for the last several minutes directly over the coals, being careful not to burn them. If you are using a barbecue glaze, apply the glaze during the last 15 minutes of cooking, until the glaze coats the wings and solidifies.

Barbecuing Tips To cook wings on the grill, I recommend that you leave on the small wing joint. Although the tips are liable to get burned, the wings are more manageable—and less likely to fall through the grates in your grill. If you are after appearance as well as taste, go ahead and remove the small wing joint; but some people happen to like the crispy, burnt end of the whole wing. I have heard some people actually parboil their wings prior to cooking them on the grill. Never do this. With certain meats, this can be beneficial, but it isn't recommended for poultry.

For charcoal grills, always presoak your charcoal with lighter fluid for at least 5 minutes before you light it.

Buy a good meat thermometer, and be sure to cook your wings to a minimum of 170 degrees. Measure the temperature by placing the thermometer into the fattest part of the wing.

BAKING

When it comes to cooking steaks or chicken, there is really nothing that can compare to the true barbecue flavor that comes straight off the grill. Luckily, wings are the ideal oven food—perfect for anyone without access to a grill. Almost any of the recipes in this book that call for a grill can be cooked in the oven instead, using the following simple instructions.

Method for Baking Wings Using a paper towel, lightly oil a 9 × 13-inch baking sheet to prevent wings from sticking. Place your prepared wings in a single layer on the prepared baking sheet and bake in a preheated 350 degree oven until crisp and brown, 30 to 40 minutes. If you are using a marinade, you can periodically baste the wings for the first 15 minutes. If you are applying a barbecue glaze, apply during the last 10 minutes of cooking. For extra-crispy wings, you may place the wings under the broiler for 2 or 3 minutes at the end of cooking.

Method for Broiling Wings The fastest way to cook wings in the oven is to broil them. To broil, place wings on a heavy 9 × 13-inch baking sheet 6 or 7 inches from the broiler and cook, turning frequently, for 8 minutes, or until juices are clear when chicken is poked with a knife. You will want to have a nice, long pair of tongs for this.

A NOTE ON SERVING SIZES

As a general rule for wings, $3\frac{1}{2}$ to 4 pounds of wings should give you twenty to thirty wings, enough to serve four to six people a hearty appetizer-sized portion. Chicken wings do vary in size. For our purposes, when I indicate thirty chicken wings, I am talking about a "medium"-sized wing in which the wing tip has been removed. You may also substitute a "drumette," or the small drumsticks that often come packaged with wings in the supermarket. In addition, when I suggest that thirty wings "serves six," I am assuming that five fairly decent-sized wings constitutes a reasonable appetizer-sized portion. Some people, myself included, tend to eat many, many more than five or six wings at a sitting—appetizer or not. Adjust accordingly.

SUPERBOWL
CLASSIC
WINGS

These are the wings you know and love—wings served in a mountainous heap, preferably alongside a pint of your favorite pub ale with the football game steadily marking off time on the television. Whether they are deep-fried and dunked in a cold pool of tangy blue cheese dressing, or piping hot Atomic wings that make your nose run and eyes water, these are the time-tested classics! If you absolutely have to have the original recipe that started it all, try reliving history by making the original Anchor Bar Wings from Buffalo, New York (page 24). Or, try the Classic Buffalo Wings recipe (page 26)—my distillation of the past thirty years in improvements to the original. For summer, break out the grill and try making one of the barbecue recipes with a classic barbecue sauce or glaze. Whatever recipe you choose, just remember to grab a fistful of extra napkins, and enjoy. . . .

This is one of many "authentic" recipes for the original Buffalo wing invented by Teressa Bellissimo in 1964, and the progenitor of all Buffalo wing recipes to follow. What I consider the key to this recipe is the use of margarine (never butter) in the sauce. The margarine acts as a sort of lubricant, helping to coat each wing with the delicious mixture of hot sauce and spices. By the way, the original recipe calls for Frank's RedHot—not Tabasco—pepper sauce. To be truly authentic, serve this with an ice-cold Genesee Cream Ale, an upstate New York tradition.

SERVES 6

Deep-fry the well-dried wings in vegetable oil in batches of 12 to 15 wings, until uniformly brown, about 15 minutes (see page 16 for more information). Drain the wings completely of residual oil. In a large saucepan over a medium flame, mix together the hot sauce, margarine, vinegar, Worcestershire sauce, cayenne, red pepper flakes, celery seed, garlic salt, and black pepper. Heat until the margarine is melted and the ingredients are well combined. Remove from heat and pour the mixture over the wings. Cover the bowl with plastic wrap or aluminum foil. Shake the bowl to cover the wings with the sauce. Serve with celery sticks and blue cheese dressing on the side.

30 chicken wings, small wing joint removed
Oil for deep-frying

6 tablespoons Frank's RedHot Cayenne Pepper Sauce
$1/4$ cup ($1/2$ stick) margarine
1 tablespoon white vinegar
1 teaspoon Worcestershire sauce
$1/4$ teaspoon cayenne pepper
$1/4$ teaspoon red pepper flakes
$1/8$ teaspoon celery seed
$1/8$ teaspoon garlic salt
1 dash black pepper
Celery sticks, for serving
Blue Cheese Dressing (use Marie's, available in your local supermarket, or see page 26 for recipe), for serving

You hear a lot about "atomic" wings in bars and restaurants. These wings are advertised as so ridiculously hot that they actually cause your eyes to water, your nose to run, your tongue to catch fire—and, more than likely, give you a king-sized case of heartburn. Most of the time, these "atomic" wings turn out to be not very hot, and not very good. So, at last, here's a way to make wings that will please your friends with a penchant for pepper. The key to making super-spicy and hot wings is both the amount and type of hot sauce you use. If you stick with Tabasco, the recipe can be adjusted easily by adding more. However, with certain "insanity" hot sauces, a mere dash can add as much heat as half a bottle of the off-the-shelf variety. (For a guide to hot sauces, see page 12.) It's easy and fun to experiment, if only to find out your pain threshold, but I've always found this recipe hot enough for me.

SERVES 6

Preheat the oven to 375 degrees. Make the wing glaze by combining in a large mixing bowl the brown sugar, vinegar, oil, hot sauces, garlic powder, cumin, chile powder, and red pepper flakes. Taste the glaze, and adjust the heat to taste by adding hot sauce until the desired level of heat is reached. Place the wings on a large baking sheet and, using a pastry brush, thoroughly coat the wings with the glaze. Bake for 15 to 20 minutes, until crisp. Serve with homemade blue cheese dressing and the ubiquitous celery sticks on the side.

NOTE Scoville units range from 0 to 16,000,000. A sauce that boasts above 5,000 should suffice for all but the most hardcore of pepperheads.

30 chicken wings, small wing joint removed

$\frac{1}{4}$ cup brown sugar

1 tablespoon white vinegar

2 tablespoons vegetable oil

3 tablespoons Tabasco or Frank's RedHot Cayenne Pepper Sauce

1 tablespoon hot sauce (try Dave's "Insanity" or a sauce equally high in Scoville units; see Note)

$\frac{1}{4}$ teaspoon garlic powder

$\frac{1}{4}$ teaspoon ground cumin

$\frac{1}{4}$ teaspoon mild pure chile powder

$\frac{1}{4}$ teaspoon red pepper flakes

1 cup Blue Cheese Dressing (page 26)

Celery sticks, for serving

CLASSIC BUFFALO WINGS

In this crunchier take on the classic Buffalo wing recipe, the wings are marinated in hot sauce prior to being dredged in spicy flour and deep-fried. An extra coating of flour gives them a beautiful uniform, golden brown appearance, and the wonderful crunch evocative of Southern-style fried chicken. This recipe also calls for you to make your own blue cheese dipping sauce, which is quite simple—and fun to experiment with. Try substituting Gorgonzola or any other blue cheese you like (Roquefort, Maytag, Stilton) and you will be surprised at the results!

SERVES 6

Place the wings in a glass or other nonreactive bowl and add 1 cup of the hot sauce. Mix thoroughly, being sure all the wings are coated, cover, and refrigerate for a minimum of 30 minutes.

Place the flour in a separate mixing bowl and season with kosher salt and cayenne pepper to taste. In a separate bowl, prepare an egg wash by whisking together the eggs and milk until well blended. Working with all three bowls (wings, flour mixture, and egg wash), first dredge each wing in the flour mixture; then dip the wing into the egg wash; and finally dredge the wing completely in the flour mixture, coating it evenly. Deep-fry the wings for 12 to 15 minutes, or until the batter achieves a crisp, uniform texture (see page 16 for more information). When cooked through, set aside to drain on paper towels or the nonprinted side of a paper grocery bag.

30 chicken wings, small wing joint removed

2 cups hot sauce
1/4 teaspoon Worcestershire sauce
1 1/2 cups flour
Kosher salt
Cayenne pepper
2 large eggs
1/4 cup whole milk
Oil for deep-frying

BLUE CHEESE DRESSING
1 cup sour cream
1/2 cup mayonnaise
Juice of 1 lemon
1 tablespoon white vinegar
1/4 cup chopped parsley
1 teaspoon minced shallots
1/2 teaspoon minced garlic
1/4 pound blue cheese, crumbled

Celery sticks, for serving

To make the Blue Cheese Dressing, in a mixing bowl and using a wire whisk, combine the sour cream, mayonnaise, lemon juice, vinegar, parsley, shallots, and garlic, blending until smooth. Gently stir in the crumbled cheese until completely mixed in.

To serve, place the fried wings in a large bowl and drench with the remaining 1 cup hot sauce (or less, to taste). Serve with the blue cheese dipping sauce and celery sticks on the side—and plenty of napkins!

MAHOGANY

Of course, not all wings need to be of the "Buffalo" or "atomic" variety. These classic mahogany wings are delicious and easy to prepare. In this recipe, you'll make a simple twenty-four-hour marinade using plum sauce, hoisin sauce, soy sauce, chili, and the garlic mixture also known as Peking sauce. These sweet and spicy wings are the perfect accompaniment to a Thai salad or a bowl of miso soup.

SEE PHOTOGRAPH ON PAGE 30.

SERVES 6

In a large bowl, combine the plum sauce, hoisin sauce, soy sauce, vinegar, sherry, honey, scallions, and garlic. Reserve $1/2$ cup of the mixture for basting in a separate small bowl. Add the chicken wings to the large bowl, stir to coat, and place, covered, in the refrigerator for a minimum of 2 hours—preferably overnight. Place the wings in a single layer on a large baking sheet. Place them in a preheated 350 degree oven and bake for 30 to 40 minutes, until crisp and brown. Baste every 10 minutes during cooking, and about 5 minutes before removing the wings from the oven.

$3/4$ cup Chinese plum sauce

$1/2$ cup Chinese hoisin sauce

$1/2$ cup soy sauce (or a low-sodium version, if preferred)

$1/3$ cup apple cider vinegar

$1/4$ cup dry sherry

$1/4$ cup honey

5 scallions, green and white parts, finely minced

6 garlic cloves, finely minced

30 chicken wings, small wing joint removed

Here is a great way to spice up baked chicken wings that is crowd pleasing and easily prepared with ingredients found in most pantries. Baked, breaded wings go from plain to extraordinary when Parmesan cheese, sesame seeds, and a few basic spices are simply included in the mix. Make them even better by serving these versatile wings with Jalapeño Dipping Sauce or Sweet-and-Sour Dipping Sauce.

SEE PHOTOGRAPH ON PAGE 31.

SERVES 4 TO 6

EASY SESAME WINGS

Preheat oven to 350 degrees.

In a small saucepan, lightly toast the sesame seeds over a high flame until they are slightly golden. Set aside.

In a microwave or in a small saucepan over low heat, melt the butter. Pour it into a bowl and set aside.

In a large plastic bag, combine the bread crumbs, Parmesan, sesame seeds, and spices. Shake well, until well mixed.

To coat the wings, dip them into the melted butter, shake off any excess, place the wings in the bag, and shake until coated (do this in batches of 3 to 5 wings at a time). Bake according to the method described on page 20, until golden brown. Serve with Jalapeño Dipping Sauce or Sweet-and-Sour Dipping Sauce .

$1/2$ cup sesame seeds
$3/4$ cup ($1 1/2$ sticks) unsalted butter
$1 1/2$ cups plain bread crumbs
$3/4$ cup grated Parmesan cheese
$3/4$ teaspoon cayenne pepper
$1/2$ teaspoon salt
$1/2$ teaspoon freshly ground black pepper
$1/4$ teaspoon onion powder

30 chicken wings, jointed and small wing joint removed
Jalapeño Dipping Sauce (page 85; optional)
Sweet-and-Sour Dipping Sauce (page 90; optional)

OPPOSITE: Mahogany Wings, page 28. ABOVE: Easy Sesame Wings, page 29

Here's another favorite recipe that combines an easy-to-prepare herb marinade with a classic lemon mayonnaise that can be quickly prepared on the grill or under the broiler. The fun of experimenting with chicken marinades is that they are nearly impossible to botch; if you think the flavors in your mixture will work together, they usually do. Although you can use any of the herbs in their dried form, you will be surprised at the difference fresh herbs make in your marinade—especially fresh, fragrant rosemary.

SERVES 6

Using a microplane or other fine grater, grate just the zest of half a lemon into a large non-reactive bowl. Juice the lemons into the bowl. Add the remaining marinade ingredients and mix well. Set aside 1 cup of the marinade. Place the chicken in the bowl or combine it with the marinade in a large plastic bag, making sure all the pieces are tightly covered, and refrigerate for a minimum of 2 hours, preferably overnight.

Grill the wings according to the method discussed on page 19, basting frequently with the reserved marinade. Serve with the mayonnaise on the side.

MARINADE

2 lemons

$1/2$ cup white wine

$1/2$ cup virgin olive oil

3 large garlic cloves, finely minced

4 tablespoons chopped fresh parsley

1 teaspoon minced fresh oregano

1 teaspoon minced fresh thyme

$1/2$ teaspoon kosher salt

$1/2$ teaspoon fresh rosemary

$1/4$ teaspoon cayenne pepper

$1/4$ teaspoon coarsely ground black pepper

30 chicken wings, small wing joint removed

Lemon Mayonnaise (page 89)

Sometimes when it comes to wings, simpler is better. And what could be simpler than coming home, grabbing some premarinated wings out of the refrigerator, and putting them on the grill for a treat that takes only minutes to prepare? The key to great grilling is usually found in the marinade, and the following recipe is a very good template for a chicken marinade that can be used for whatever type of chicken or poultry you're going to grill—from wings to a whole bird. The best part of making marinades is that you just can't screw them up, so open the spice rack and let your imagination run wild!

SERVES 6

In a large bowl, combine the vinegar, beer, soy sauce, lemon juice, sugar, garlic, onion, and dry spices; mix well. Add the chicken to the bowl or combine it with the marinade in a large leakproof plastic bag, reserving 1 cup of the marinade in a separate covered container and making sure the wings are completely covered (if you need more liquid, you can add warm water or more beer). Cover tightly and refrigerate overnight.

When ready to grill, bring your barbecue to a steady heat (approximately 350 degrees) and cook, lid down, for 25 to 30 minutes, or until the wings have a crispy, browned appearance. Liberally apply the reserved marinade throughout cooking, and sear the wings for the last several minutes directly over the coals, being careful not to burn them.

"ALL-PURPOSE" CHICKEN MARINADE

1 cup cider vinegar
12 ounces (1 can) beer
$\frac{1}{2}$ cup low-sodium soy sauce
Juice of 2 lemons
2 teaspoons granulated sugar
4 large garlic cloves, crushed
1 medium onion, minced
$\frac{1}{4}$ teaspoon paprika
$\frac{1}{4}$ teaspoon white pepper
$\frac{1}{4}$ teaspoon Colman's dry mustard

30 chicken wings, small wing joint removed

WIDE WORLD OF
WINGS

These days, it seems that even the humble American "family restaurant" is pushing cuisine laden with sophisticated international flavors. Not long ago, cuisine from Asia and the Subcontinent was cutting-edge. Now, you're as likely to find pad Thai and curry next to burgers and fries in the food court at the mall. Since we all seem to have acquired more than a glancing familiarity with the flavors of the Far East, it is appropriate that we enjoy the occasional wing with an international filigree. America isn't the only chicken wing–obsessed culture, after all. There are as many wing variations around the world as there are cuisines, and in this chapter, you will find a small retrospective of far-flung favorites.

KOREAN SESAME CHICKEN WINGS

Did you ever taste the sesame beef at a Korean restaurant? You wonder how they get the beef so crispy on the outside and so moist and tender on the inside. The key is the batter, which is used as a marinade also. This simple recipe also calls for beef Dashida, a Korean spice mixture found in many recipes, which is in many specialty stores. If you cannot find it, however, the recipe is still quite tasty without it.

SERVES 4

In a small, dry saucepan, roast the sesame seeds over a high flame until they are golden. In a bowl large enough to hold the chicken wings, combine the sesame seeds with the rest of the marinade ingredients and blend well. Add the chicken to the batter, turning to coat each individual piece. Marinate the wings in the refrigerator for at least 3 hours and up to overnight.

When ready to cook, remove the wings, shake off the excess batter, and discard the marinade. Deep-fry according to the method described on page 16, removing the wings after 10 to 12 minutes, after the batter has achieved a uniform, crunchy consistency.

MARINADE

2 tablespoons sesame seeds
1/2 cup cornstarch
1/4 cup flour
1/4 cup granulated sugar
5 teaspoons soy sauce
1 teaspoon beef Dashida Korean
   spice mixture
1 teaspoon salt
2 garlic cloves, finely chopped
2 scallions, white part only, finely
   chopped
2 large eggs, beaten

20 chicken wings, jointed and small
   wing joint removed
Oil for deep frying

Teriyaki is nothing more than beef or chicken that has been marinated in a mixture of sake, soy sauce, sugar, ginger, and garlic before cooking. Making authentic teriyaki sauce is very simple—and so much better than the kind you can purchase in the ethnic foods aisle of your local grocery store. Once you've tasted this great marinade, you'll want to try it on steaks, whole chicken, and even pork. The key is to let the marinade sink into the wings, so be sure to refrigerate them for 24 hours.

SERVES 6

In a large saucepan over a medium-low flame, heat the water, soy sauce, and sake until warm. Add the rest of the marinade ingredients and stir until the sugar is entirely dissolved, about 2 minutes. Remove from the heat and let stand until the marinade reaches room temperature. Place the chicken in a large bowl and pour the marinade over. Seal tightly, and keep in the refrigerator for 24 hours, or at least overnight.

Grill according to the method described on page 19, basting frequently.

TERIYAKI MARINADE

1 cup water

1 cup soy sauce

$\frac{1}{2}$ cup dry sake (or dry sherry)

$\frac{1}{4}$ cup Worcestershire sauce

$\frac{1}{4}$ cup granulated sugar

$\frac{1}{4}$ cup brown sugar

3 tablespoons vegetable oil

$\frac{1}{3}$ cup minced onion

2 teaspoons garlic powder

$\frac{1}{2}$ teaspoon ground ginger

30 chicken wings, small wing joint removed

GRILLED
JAPANESE TERIYAKI WINGS

GRILLED COCONUT WINGS

WITH THAI PEANUT DIPPING SAUCE

The secret to making authentic Thai wings is the overnight galangal and chile marinade. Used in Thai cooking, galangal is similar to ginger, and the key spice in many Thai coconut milk–based soups. Here, galangal is combined with turmeric (another close cousin to ginger), coconut milk, garlic, and hot chiles to create wings that have that authentic, spicy Thai flavor. Cool them off with a classic Thai peanut dipping sauce. Galangal can be difficult to find, but don't worry. Simply substitute ½ teaspoon of freshly grated ginger for the ground galangal, and your guests will never know.

SERVES 4

To make the marinade, using a food processor, grind the ingredients into a paste the consistency of thin yogurt. Reserve a small amount for basting and transfer the remaining marinade to a glass bowl. Add the cleaned and trimmed chicken wings. Toss liberally, cover with plastic wrap, and marinate in the refrigerator overnight.

To grill the wings, shake off the excess marinade and grill the wings over medium heat for approximately 5 minutes per side, or until crispy. Brush them frequently with the reserved marinade, and be careful not to burn the wing tips. The wings should have a crispy texture with a deep mahogany color when done.

Serve with the Thai Peanut Sauce.

MARINADE

2 cups coconut milk

1 medium onion, coarsely chopped

2 tablespoons crushed garlic

2 teaspoons ground turmeric

2 teaspoons red pepper flakes

1 teaspoon ground galangal (or ½ teaspoon freshly grated ginger)

1 tablespoon kosher salt

20 chicken wings, jointed
Thai Peanut Sauce (page 91)

JAPANESE-STYLE CHICKEN WINGS

The key to this Japanese specialty is the *jeshinko* batter, which makes for particularly crispy deep-fried chicken. Jeshinko is rice flour, which can be found at any ethnic market or specialty food store. For the authentic Japanese experience, try deep-frying these wings in a wok. Woks are the perfect deep-frying cookware, as the high sides prevent splatter, and the deep bowl shape means you need a lot less oil to cook with. If you want to avoid deep-frying altogether, you can skip the batter and grill the marinated wings on the barbecue. Wings always go better with a dipping sauce, and this Japanese Peanut Sauce is the perfect accompaniment to these battered beauties.

SERVES 6

In a large bowl, mix together the soy sauce, sesame oil, sugar, sherry, ginger, salt, hoisin sauce, and garlic until well-blended.

Place the chicken in the bowl and coat all pieces evenly with the mixture. Cover and marinate in the refrigerator for a minimum of 2 hours, and up to overnight.

About an hour prior to cooking, prepare the batter by beating the eggs, then stir in the rice flour, sugar, garlic, and soy sauce in a large mixing bowl. Cover and refrigerate for 1 hour.

To make the Japanese Peanut Sauce, combine the peanut butter, lime juice, soy sauce, prepared miso, sugar, ginger, garlic, and red pepper flakes, mixing thoroughly so that the peanut butter is fully incorporated and the sugar completely dissolved. You may

MARINADE

$\frac{1}{4}$ cup soy sauce

1 tablespoon dark sesame oil

2 teaspoons granulated sugar

2 tablespoons sherry

1 teaspoon grated fresh ginger

1 teaspoon salt

4 teaspoons hoisin sauce

3 garlic cloves, passed through a garlic press

30 chicken wings, small wing joint removed

Oil for deep-frying

BATTER

2 eggs

$\frac{1}{4}$ cup rice flour

$\frac{1}{4}$ cup granulated sugar

(CONTINUES)

store this sauce in the refrigerator for up to a week in a sealed container.

When ready to cook, remove the wings from the marinade and pat dry. Dip each piece into the batter mixture and coat thoroughly. Deep-fry according to one of the methods described on page 16, then drain well before serving with the Japanese Peanut Sauce.

BATTER (CONTINUED)

3 garlic cloves, finely minced
2 tablespoons soy sauce
2 tablespoons sesame seeds
2 tablespoons vegetable oil
3 tablespoons chopped scallions, green and white parts
2 tablespoons cornstarch

JAPANESE PEANUT SAUCE

2 tablespoons smooth peanut butter
$1/2$ cup lime juice
2 tablespoons soy sauce (low-sodium preferable)
2 teaspoons prepared miso (available in specialty stores)
4 tablespoons granulated sugar
2 teaspoons finely chopped fresh ginger
2 teaspoons finely chopped garlic
$1/2$ teaspoon dried red pepper flakes

In this spicy, crunchy recipe, ground-up tortilla chips create an irresistible coating for baked wings, filled with the the traditional chile and cumin flavors found south of the border.

SERVES 6

Preheat the oven to 375 degrees. Oil a large baking sheet.

Using a food processor or blender, pulverize the tortilla chips until finely ground, then place them in a bowl. In a separate bowl, whisk together the corn oil, chile powder, oregano, cumin, cayenne pepper, paprika, and black pepper. Dip the wings into the oil mixture, let excess oil drip off, then dredge them in the tortilla coating. Place coated wings on a large oiled baking sheet, and bake for 35 to 40 minutes following the method described on page 20, until the tortilla coating is browned and uniformly crispy.

36 ounces plain tortilla chips
1½ cups corn oil
¼ cup mild chile powder
3 teaspoons dried oregano
3 teaspoons ground cumin
1 teaspoon cayenne pepper
1 teaspoon paprika
½ teaspoon freshly ground black pepper

30 chicken wings, small wing joint removed

PAN-SEARED WINGS
WITH CLASSIC OYSTER SAUCE

Almost everyone has a go-to recipe for wings tucked away in a recipe card file or on a stained scrap of paper buried between the pages of a dog-eared copy of *The Joy of Cooking*. This particular gem was brought to my attention by Jane Treuhaft, the designer of this book, whose mother Ellie remembers the original recipe as a thin clipping from a yellowed newspaper. Modified over the years as it periodically emerged from the well-worn recipe file, this classic and easy-to-prepare recipe has become one of my favorites. I've nicknamed them "Ellie's Wings."

SERVES 4

In a mixing bowl, whisk together the oyster sauce, garlic cloves, water, and sugar; set aside.

Heat a medium-size saucepan over a medium-high flame and add the oil. When the oil is hot, place the wings in the pan and sauté until well browned, about 5 minutes. Add the sauce mixture, being careful to avoid oil splatter, and simmer over medium heat for 10 to 15 minutes.

6 tablespoons prepared oyster sauce
4 garlic cloves, crushed
2 cups water
2 tablespoons granulated sugar
5 tablespoons vegetable oil

30 chicken wings, small wing joint removed

There is an old Cantonese proverb that says, "Anything that walks, swims, crawls, or flies with its back to heaven is edible." I don't know if chickens fly with their backs to heaven or not, but I know that Cantonese food is heaven on earth. Epitomized by a reliance on fresh ingredients and a focus on preserving the natural flavor of food, authentic Cantonese cuisine bears little resemblance to the "Cantonese" food found in your local Chinese wok shop. Luckily for the wing connoisseur, the light, healthy Cantonese cooking style makes for an exceptional wing.

SERVES 6

In a bowl large enough to accommodate the wings, mix together the soy sauce, rice wine, sugar, sesame oil, garlic, and ginger. Add the wings and toss, making sure all the wings are coated, seal the bowl tightly, and place in the refrigerator overnight.

Prior to cooking, remove the wings from the marinade and add the beaten eggs to the marinade. Resoak the wings in the marinade briefly, then dredge them in the cornstarch, making sure to coat each wing thoroughly. Deep-fry the wings according to the method described on page 16. Serve hot with warm teriyaki marinade on the side.

MARINADE

$\frac{1}{4}$ cup low-sodium soy sauce

3 tablespoons rice wine (or sherry)

2 teaspoons granulated sugar

2 teaspoons toasted sesame oil

4 garlic cloves, minced

1 2-inch piece of fresh ginger, minced

30 chicken wings, small wing joint removed

Oil for deep-frying

BATTER

2 large eggs

2 cups cornstarch

Teriyaki Marinade (page 37)

CANTONESE-STYLE BARBECUED WINGS

About six hundred miles west of China's east coast, Szechwan Province is famous for its cuisine. Szechwan dishes are the hottest and spiciest of the four main types of Chinese cuisine (Shanghai, Peking, and Cantonese being the others), with many of the dishes getting their fiery flavor from chile peppers. This easy recipe evokes the flavor of traditional Szechwan cuisine by combining ginger, garlic, and hot chile peppers to really heat things up.

SERVES 6

2 oranges
$1/2$ cup low-sodium soy sauce
6 tablespoons toasted sesame oil
2 garlic cloves, minced
2 scallions, chopped
1 teaspoon granulated sugar
1 teaspoon brown sugar
30 chicken wings
2 small jalapeño peppers, seeded and finely chopped
$3^1/2$ teaspoons cornstarch

Grate the orange to produce about 2 tablespoons of zest. Cut the oranges in half and juice them into a medium-size bowl. Add the soy sauce, sesame oil, garlic, scallions, and granulated and brown sugars; mix well.

Place the chicken wings on a large platter and coat them with a generous amount of the marinade. Cover tightly and refrigerate overnight. Grill the wings according to the method described on page 19, basting the wings frequently during cooking.

After the wings are grilled, place the remaining sauce in a small saucepan, add the jalapeños, and cook over high heat until simmering. Lower the heat and gradually whisk in the cornstarch. Simmer until the sauce is thickened, then remove from the heat and serve as a dipping sauce on the side.

One of my favorite Indian dishes is chicken vindaloo, the super-spicy dish that my English-challenged former colleague Shah likes to describe as "very too hot." These delicious curry wings are not vindaloo strength, but you can ratchet up the heat by adding cayenne pepper to the marinade, which is a thick, chutney-based "wet rub" that will infuse the wings with delicious subcontinental flavors and crisp up to perfection in the oven. The yogurt dipping sauce substitutes for traditional blue cheese dressing, providing a cooling and delicious accompaniment.

SERVES 6

To prepare the marinade, in a large bowl whisk together the curry powder, chutney, lemon juice, seasoned salt, cayenne pepper, and paprika. Coat each wing with the mixture, seal the wings in a large plastic bag, and refrigerate overnight—or up to 24 hours if possible.

Preheat the oven to 375 degrees. In a small bowl, mix the soy sauce and water and set aside for basting the wings. On a large, ungreased baking sheet, bake the wings according to the method described on page 20, basting frequently with the soy sauce mixture.

Meanwhile, prepare the dipping sauce: Place the yogurt in a small bowl, and coarsely grate the cucumbers into the yogurt. Pass the garlic clove through a garlic press into the bowl and stir in the olive oil, dill, and white pepper. Serve chilled on the side.

30 chicken wings, small wing joint removed

CURRY "WET RUB"
1/4 cup mild curry powder
1/4 cup prepared mango chutney
1/4 cup freshly squeezed lemon juice
1 teaspoon seasoned salt
1/2 teaspoon cayenne pepper
1/4 teaspoon paprika
2 tablespoons soy sauce
2 tablespoons water

YOGURT-DILL DIPPING SAUCE
1 cup plain yogurt, chilled
2 cucumbers, peeled and seeded
1 garlic clove
2 teaspoons olive oil
1 1/2 teaspoons dried dill
1/2 teaspoon white pepper

There is nothing like the taste of chicken baked in a tandoor, the traditional Indian clay oven. In tandoor cooking, a large clay jar is buried in the earth and heated by white-hot coals. Meat is threaded on long skewers and lowered into the clay oven, which evenly distributes the heat from the coals, roasting the meat to perfection. The combination of barbecued flavor and the rich taste of exotic Indian spices make Tandoori chicken a true specialty. If you don't have access to a tandoor, this dish can be made in your oven in a regular baking pan without sacrificing too much of the authentic flavor.

SERVES 6

In a bowl large enough to accommodate the chicken, combine the grated ginger, pressed garlic, and dry spices (except turmeric) with the yogurt and vegetable oil. Add the chicken wings, coating each piece completely. Marinate, covered with plastic wrap, overnight.

When ready to cook, preheat the oven to 350 degrees, remove the chicken from the marinade, and place on an oiled baking pan. Sprinkle the chicken with turmeric and bake for 35 to 40 minutes, basting frequently, until the chicken's juices run clear when you poke the meaty section with a fork.

1 tablespoon peeled and grated fresh ginger
4 large garlic cloves, passed through a garlic press
1 teaspoon cumin seeds
$1/4$ teaspoon cayenne pepper
$1/4$ teaspoon salt
$1/4$ teaspoon ground nutmeg
$1/4$ teaspoon ground cinnamon
$1/8$ teaspoon ground cloves
1 cup plain yogurt
3 tablespoons vegetable oil
30 chicken wings, small wing joint removed
$1/2$ teaspoon ground turmeric

TANDOORI WINGS

BARBECUED THAI CHICKEN WINGS

Here is a simpler take on Thai-style chicken wings, inspired by the street vendors who hawk their wares on the corners of Bangkok. To make this recipe, you'll need to find Thai chile paste. Try *sambal oelek,* a traditional Thai chile paste that doesn't contain garlic, onions, spices, or other additives—just pure chiles. If you can't find that, go to the ethnic food store and search for a sauce called Ta-Dang (literally, "red-eye") on the label, and you'll be in good shape. Failing that, you can easily make it yourself (see below). The key to these wings is a long marinade; try and keep the wings soaking for at least twenty-four hours to allow the wonderful flavors of lemongrass, cilantro, and chile to mingle and penetrate the meat.

SERVES 4 TO 6

In a large bowl, combine the marinade ingredients. Add the chicken wings, cover, and marinate for at least 2 hours, and up to overnight. Grill the wings using the method described on page 19, remembering to baste the wings frequently during cooking.

SAMBAL OELEK

If you need to make your own Thai chile paste, combine the 1/4 pound stemmed red chiles, 1 teaspoon kosher salt, and about 1 teaspoon white wine vinegar in a food processor and process until a smooth paste forms, about 3 minutes. Adjust thickness with vinegar.

MARINADE

1/2 cup coarsely chopped lemongrass

1/2 cup finely chopped cilantro

6 large garlic cloves, passed through a garlic press

2 tablespoons purchased *sambal oelek* (Ta-Dang), or see below

2 teaspoons ground turmeric

2 teaspoons kosher salt

30 chicken wings

NOTE The key to safe chile preparation is to wear rubber gloves when handling chiles. When cutting the peppers, be gentle so as to avoid squirting the volatile oil into your eyes. And avoid touching your nose, mouth, or eyes. When reconstituting dried chiles, be sure to use only cold water, as the steam from hot water can collect the oils and transfer them into your nose and eyes. Always wash your hands before and especially after handling chiles (even if you wear gloves). If your skin starts burning, try wiping your hands with a paper towel moistened with clear vinegar.

In Latin America, *chiccarrón* literally means "pork rinds," the crispy deep-fried pork skins popular across Central America and the Caribbean. Unlike the salty, bagged variety of pork rinds you can find in your local ethnic food market or bodega, freshly prepared *chiccarrén*—bite-sized pork skins fried in lard—is popular for its wonderful crunch. These wings get their name from the texture of the chicken skin when deep-fried without batter; they are wonderfully crunchy, with delicious, moist deep-marinated chicken underneath. The best part of the wing to prepare this way is the small "drumette" portion of the wing, which looks like a miniature drumstick.

SERVES 6

In a bowl large enough to accommodate the wings, combine the marinade ingredients, mixing thoroughly. Add the chicken to the mixture, cover, and refrigerate for 24 hours.

Preheat the oven to 375 degrees. Bake according to the method described on page 20, basting the drumettes frequently. When done, deep-fry the wings in batches until crunchy, about 2 minutes. If you cannot deep-fry the wings, place them under the broiler for 2 to 3 minutes. Serve with the Jalapeño Dipping Sauce.

MARINADE

5 large garlic cloves
2 teaspoons salt
3 teaspoons onion powder
3 teaspoons freshly ground black
    pepper
2 tablespoons paprika
3 teaspoons dried oregano
2 tablespoons ground coriander
$1/2$ cup peanut oil
$1/2$ cup low-sodium chicken stock
$1/3$ cup white wine vinegar
$1/2$ cup hot pepper sauce, or to taste
Juice of 5 limes

30 chicken-wing drumettes
Oil for deep-frying
Jalapeño Dipping Sauce (page 85)

I know of no better sauce for meat than this South American one—the vinegar-based, herb-infused sauce served at almost every Argentinian and Brazilian road-side grilled-meat joint. Use this sauce to baste wings during cooking, and serve it as a dipping sauce for barbecued wings.

SERVES 6

This recipe is staggeringly easy to prepare. First, get a pot large enough to hold the ingredients. In a separate pot, bring the water to a raging boil. Following the list of ingredients in order, place each into the large pot—the garlic, followed by the parsley, oregano, and dried pepper. Pour the boiling water on top, and then add the vinegar, olive oil, salt, and pepper. Let cool for about an hour. Transfer the mixture to a covered jar and store in the refrigerator for at least 24 hours to let the flavors blend. It can be stored this way for up to 14 days.

On a medium-hot barbecue grill, cook the wings over indirect heat (covered) for approximately 20 minutes. Finish the wings by placing directly over the heat and searing for 5 minutes, until the wings are slightly charcoaled. Baste liberally. Serve hot off the grill with the dipping sauce on the side, and plenty of ice-cold pilsner-style beer.

1 cup water
8 large garlic cloves, finely minced
1/2 cup finely chopped parsley
1/2 cup finely chopped fresh oregano
1/4 cup dried red pepper flakes
1/2 cup white wine vinegar
1/2 cup extra-virgin olive oil
1 teaspoon salt
1 teaspoon freshly ground black pepper

30 chicken wings

WITH TRADITIONAL SOUTH AMERICAN VINEGAR AND HERB SAUCE

GOURMET
WINGS

Maybe it's the abundance of food programming on cable television, but it's hard to resist the occasional urge to go beyond your standard core of recipes and attempt to create a truly "gourmet" dish in your own kitchen. Before you know it, you're splashing the wine and spices around the kitchen like a junior version of Alain Ducasse. Let's face it. Any fry jockey can make a heaping plate of wings that surpasses the offering at your local TGI Friday's, but it takes a little bit of extra finesse to turn the garden-variety wing into a work of culinary genius. Here are some recipes that even the most jaded, *Zagat*-owning "foodie" would be hard-pressed to turn up his nose at.

OVEN-BAKED WINGS

WITH ROSEMARY SHALLOT GLAZE

More flavorful than onions and subtler than garlic, shallots are perfect for making sauces and glazes for wings, as they will not overpower the flavor of the chicken. This rosemary shallot glaze is quick and easy to prepare—and wonderful for any chicken dish, whether oven-baked or grilled.

SERVES 6

Preheat the oven to 375 degrees.

In a medium-size saucepan, heat the oil over medium-high heat. Add the butter. When the butter is melted, add the shallots and rosemary and sauté until the shallots are softened, about 4 minutes. Add the water, lemon juice, sugar, salt, and pepper. Reduce heat to low and simmer until the sauce is slightly thickened, about 10 minutes. Remove from the heat and allow to cool for 15 to 20 minutes.

Arrange the chicken wings in a shallow baking pan and coat evenly with the rosemary shallot glaze. Bake according to the method described on page 20, until the chicken skin is golden brown and crispy. Serve with a dry white wine.

$\frac{1}{4}$ cup olive oil

$\frac{1}{4}$ cup ($\frac{1}{2}$ stick) salted butter

$\frac{1}{4}$ cup finely chopped shallots

1 tablespoon dried rosemary

1 cup water

Juice of 2 lemons

1 tablespoon granulated sugar

1 teaspoon salt

2 teaspoons coarsely ground black pepper

30 chicken wings, jointed and small wing joint removed

Like American politics, the popular sentiment regarding using nuts in cooking seems to be evenly divided: You either like nuts in your food or you hate the idea. Whether you are talking about Chinese dishes, the Thanksgiving stuffing, or the crust on your Dover sole, some people just don't enjoy nuts in their food. I happen to think that adding the flavor and texture of nuts to poultry—especially succulent, crunchy almonds—makes for an undeniably more flavorful experience.

SERVES 6

Wash the wings, pat them dry, and toss them in the flour. Shake off excess flour and set aside. In a medium-size bowl, combine the eggs and milk and whisk until the eggs are slightly beaten. In a blender or food processor, grind the almonds until they are fine. Place in a large mixing bowl. In a blender or food processor grind the white bread until fine. Add the crumbs to the almonds and stir in the salt and orange zest. Dip the wings in the egg mixture, then dredge in the almond-bread mixture until well coated. Set the wings on a shallow ungreased baking pan. Fry the wings according to one of the methods described on page 16.

To make the plum sauce, heat the plum jam in a small saucepan over medium heat until melted. Stir in remaining plum sauce ingredients. Bring the mixture to a boil and cook for 1 minute, stirring constantly. Serve the wings hot with the warm plum dipping sauce on the side.

30 chicken wings, disjointed and
   small wing joint removed
1 1/2 cups flour
2 eggs, slightly beaten
2 cups milk
1 1/2 cups blanched whole almonds
10 slices stale white bread, crusts
   removed
2 teaspoons salt
4 teaspoons grated orange zest
Oil for deep-frying

PLUM SAUCE
1 cup plum jam
2 teaspoons grated lemon zest
1 tablespoon lemon juice
1 tablespoon seasoned rice vinegar
1/2 teaspoon ground ginger
1/2 teaspoon crushed anise seeds
1/4 teaspoon mustard powder
1/4 teaspoon ground cinnamon
1/8 teaspoon ground cloves
1/8 teaspoon hot pepper sauce

PARMESAN MUSTARD WINGS

One of my favorite chicken recipes was always my mother's "deviled" chicken—oven-baked chicken parts with a homemade breading infused with Parmesan cheese straight out of the Kraft jar. These homestyle wings are simple to prepare and tasty even at room temperature, which makes them perfect to pack for a picnic lunch or a trip to the beach. The secret to this recipe is using a slightly stale white bread—Wonder Bread a day past its prime is ideal.

SERVES 6

Preheat the oven to 375 degrees.

Place the bread in a blender or food processor and grind until fine, about 2 minutes. In a large mixing bowl, combine 3 cups of the bread crumbs and the Parmesan cheese, stirring until well blended. Set aside.

Using a coffee grinder or mortar and pestle, grind the mustard seeds to a coarse consistency, then put them in a large mixing bowl. Add the Dijon mustard, oil, salt, vinegar, and cayenne to the mustard powder and whisk thoroughly. Add the wings to the mixture and toss to coat evenly, pressing the wings into the mixture.

Place the wings on a large ungreased baking pan, and bake according to the method described on page 20.

10 slices white bread, crusts removed

1 1/2 cups finely grated Parmesan cheese

4 teaspoons whole mustard seeds

1 cup Dijon mustard

4 teaspoons vegetable oil

1 teaspoon salt

4 teaspoons white wine vinegar

1/2 teaspoon cayenne pepper

30 chicken wings, small wing joint removed

Even though Spam is practically Hawaii's state dish, there are more than a few Hawaiian specialties that are worth bringing back to the mainland—one of which is their excellent barbecue glazes. Although we mainly associate Hawaii with the delicious pineapple ham glazes, there is nothing like the flavor of ginger and fresh pineapple on slow-barbecued chicken.

SERVES 6

In a medium saucepan, combine the pineapple juice, vegetable oil, lemon juice, molasses, soy sauce, ground ginger, and vinegar. Simmer over medium heat until steam rises from the surface, about 5 minutes. Add the orange marmalade and pineapple preserves and stir until fully incorporated into the sauce, about 3 minutes. Let simmer until slightly reduced, about 10 minutes. Remove from the heat and let cool.

Place the chicken wings in a shallow baking pan and pour the mixture over the wings, making sure to completely coat each wing. Refrigerate for a minimum of 3 hours and preferably overnight. Slow-barbecue the wings in a covered grill over medium indirect heat for approximately 35 minutes (see page 19 for details).

¾ cup pineapple juice
½ cup vegetable oil
¼ cup lemon juice
¼ cup unsulphured molasses
⅓ cup soy sauce
1 teaspoon ground ginger
2 tablespoons white vinegar
¼ cup orange marmalade
⅓ cup pineapple preserves

30 chicken wings, small wing joint removed

This Asian-inspired recipe that combines the great flavor of sesame and ginger with spicy red pepper and zesty lime makes for delicious finger food—citrusy, sweet, and savory.

SERVES 6

To make the marinade, in a food processor or blender combine the scallions, soy sauce, lime juice, honey, lime zest, sesame oil, ginger, red pepper flakes, and garlic. Process on high speed until smooth, about 2 minutes. Pour into a large bowl and add the chicken wings. Cover well and allow to marinate overnight in the refrigerator, turning occasionally to make sure each piece is covered. Grill or bake at 375 degrees according to the methods described on pages 19 and 20. Sprinkle with sesame seeds before serving.

In the meantime, to make the Warm Lime Dipping Sauce, combine the ingredients in a saucepan and heat until warm. Serve on the side as a dipping sauce.

MARINADE

1/2 cup chopped scallions, white and green parts

1/4 cup soy sauce

1/4 cup lime juice

1/4 cup honey

3 teaspoons grated lime zest

2 1/2 teaspoons dark sesame oil

1 teaspoon ground ginger or a 1-inch piece of fresh ginger, finely grated

1/2 teaspoon red pepper flakes

4 large garlic cloves

30 wings, jointed and small wing joint removed

Sesame seeds, for garnish

WARM LIME DIPPING SAUCE

5 tablespoons lime juice

1/2 cup melted butter

1/8 teaspoon garlic powder

1/4 cup granulated sugar

1/4 cup white wine

3 tablespoons rum

Freshly ground black pepper to taste

GRILLED GINGER-LIME WINGS WITH WARM LIME DIPPING SAUCE

The reason wings are one of the most versatile dishes is their ability to stand up to a large variety of sauces. With this easy white wine dressing, simply deep-fried wings become a quick and special treat. I discovered this recipe when experimenting with a salad dressing during the summer and munching on take-out wings. Make a huge garden salad with avocados and blue cheese dressing, and serve these wings on the patio for a special summer meal.

SERVES 6

In a medium-size bowl, combine the cornstarch, white pepper, salt, and cayenne. Mix well. Moisten the chicken in water and dredge the wings in the mixture until well coated. Deep-fry according to one of the methods described on page 16 until golden brown. Set aside, uncovered.

In a large bowl, combine the extra-virgin olive oil, vinegar, wine, salt, pepper, and dried spices. Using a garlic press, crush the garlic into the mixture and blend well. Add the peppers and onion and adjust the seasoning to taste with salt and pepper. Place the chicken wings in a large shallow bowl, cover with the chardonnay dressing, and toss well, coating each wing thoroughly. Alternatively, serve the wings dry, with the chardonnay dipping sauce on the side.

1 cup cornstarch
$\frac{1}{2}$ tablespoon white pepper
$\frac{1}{2}$ tablespoon salt
1 teaspoon cayenne pepper

30 chicken wings, jointed and small
    wing joint removed
Oil for deep-frying

CHARDONNAY DRESSING
2 cups extra-virgin olive oil
1 cup white wine vinegar
$\frac{1}{2}$ cup chardonnay wine
1 teaspoon salt, or to taste
1 teaspoon coarsely ground black
    pepper, or to taste
1 teaspoon mustard powder
1 teaspoon dried basil
1 teaspoon dried oregano
1 teaspoon dried tarragon
2 garlic cloves
$\frac{1}{2}$ red bell pepper, diced
$\frac{1}{2}$ green bell pepper, diced
$\frac{1}{4}$ small white onion, diced

Just like Jamaica's famous jerk cuisine, Cajun-style cooking evolved from a little-known regional specialty to a worldwide phenomenon during a span of several years in the mid-1980s. Nowadays—BAM!—Cajun food is everywhere, from the lowliest diner to the fanciest restaurant. Cajuns are descended from French Acadians who settled in southern Louisiana in the eighteenth century. Cajun cuisine is simple country fare characterized by spices such as cayenne pepper and Creole mustard, a pungent, coarse Dijon variety. This easy recipe is full of classic Cajun flavors, and can be prepared in under an hour, too!

SERVES 6

CAJUN WINGS

Preheat the oven to 350 degrees.

In a blender, combine all of the dry spices—the bay leaves, caraway seed, cayenne, cumin, coriander, mustard powder, paprika, thyme, and salt—and pulse on a low setting until well combined. Add the Cognac and lime juice to the spice mixture. Using a garlic press, add the garlic cloves. Then stir the mixture into a paste.

Place the wings in a shallow baking pan. Using a pastry brush, coat each wing liberally with the Cajun rub, then bake for 35 to 40 minutes. The wings should emerge from the oven brown and crispy. Serve with ice-cold beer and celery sticks.

5 bay leaves
1½ teaspoons caraway seed
1½ teaspoons cayenne pepper
1½ teaspoons ground cumin
1½ teaspoons ground coriander
3 teaspoons mustard powder
3 teaspoons paprika
1½ teaspoons dried thyme leaves
1 teaspoon salt
¼ cup Cognac
¼ cup lime juice, freshly squeezed
6 large garlic cloves

30 chicken wings, wing joint
   removed
Celery sticks, for serving

PEANUT WINGS

If you are a fan of chicken satay, the Thai-style grilled chicken skewers served with peanut dipping sauce, you are sure to enjoy these crunchy peanut-coated wings hot off the grill. Most of the ingredients for this recipe can be found in your refrigerator (with the exception of sesame oil, which you can omit if you don't have it). I like to add quite a bit more hot pepper sauce in my peanut wings—something about the initial sweet flavor followed by the pleasant hot pepper sauce sting is what makes these wings so interesting to have as an appetizer. (Adjust the heat to your liking by tasting the liquid coating prior to "breading" your wings with the peanuts.)

SERVES 6

Place the peanuts in a blender or food processor and chop until finely ground, 1 or 2 minutes. Set aside.

In a medium-size bowl, combine the mustard, sour cream, peanut butter, soy sauce, hot sauce (if using), oil, ginger, and white pepper; mix until well blended. Dip the chicken wings into the liquid batter, and then into the crushed peanut topping, being sure to coat each piece thoroughly. These may be oven-baked (see page 20) or cooked on the grill (see page 19).

24 ounces peanuts, dry-roasted and unsalted
1 cup Dijon mustard
$1/2$ cup sour cream
$1/4$ cup creamy peanut butter
$1/4$ cup soy sauce
1 tablespoon Frank's RedHot Cayenne Pepper Sauce, if desired
$1/2$ teaspoon dark sesame oil
2 teaspoons ground ginger
$1/2$ teaspoon white pepper

30 chicken wings, small wing joint removed

JERK-RUBBED

It wasn't too many years ago that Jamaica's "jerk" cuisine was the latest culinary fad. Nowadays, jerk sauces are available in your local supermarket and jerk chicken and pork dishes appear often on American restaurant menus. Despite its popularity, many people don't have a great appreciation for its origins—that's why making a jerk marinade is as informative as it is fun.

Jerk started in Jamaica in the mid-1600s by slaves known as the Maroons, a West African hunting tribe. Before going wild boar hunting, which involved long journeys, they would heavily spice their meat, wrap it in leaves, and pit-smoke it for long periods of time to preserve it. Along the way, "jerk" has evolved with the many ethnic groups in Jamaica, and it is not hard to detect the subtle Asian, European, African, and East Indian influences in various regional jerk recipes.

Why is it called jerk? One theory has it that the proprietors of Jamaica's famous jerk huts would have to jerk off a piece of meat from the pork slab to serve it to customers. The secret to good jerk? Marinate it long and cook it slowly.

SERVES 6

Using rubber gloves and being careful to avoid getting pepper oil in your eyes (see page 51), remove the seeds and stems from the chile peppers and chop the peppers finely. Set the scallions, ginger, and garlic into a medium bowl. Add the vegetable oil, rum, and thyme; mix well and set aside.

In a separate bowl, combine the rest of the ingredients and mix thoroughly. Reserve enough dry rub to cover the chicken after marinating. Add the remaining spice mixture to the wet sauce and whisk together.

3 small Scotch bonnet chile peppers

1 bunch of scallions, white part only, finely chopped

A 5-inch piece of fresh ginger, peeled and finely chopped

3 large garlic cloves, minced

¼ cup vegetable oil

¼ cup dark rum (Appleton's is a good choice)

2 tablespoons finely chopped fresh thyme leaves

6 bay leaves

1 tablespoon ground allspice

(CONTINUES)

Place the wings in a large plastic bag, pour in the jerk marinade, and marinate overnight. Prior to grilling, apply a light coating of the reserved dry rub to the marinated chicken. Barbecue slowly, according to the method described on page 19.

Barbecue slowly, according to the method described on page 19.

(CONTINUED)

2 teaspoons ground nutmeg

2 teaspoons ground cinnamon

1 tablespoon ground allspice

2 tablespoons freshly ground black pepper

2 tablespoons ground coriander

1 tablespoon brown sugar

1 tablespoon kosher salt

30 chicken wings, jointed, small wing joint removed

Don't be afraid of a little garlic! Even though these wings are marinated in a garlicky brew overnight, they won't overpower you or your guests, who are guaranteed to reach for more. A simple garlic and pepper marinade, served with a delicious cool ranch dipping sauce spiced up with a bit of chile for kick, make these awesome wings perfect with a bunch of pale ale or crisp white wine.

SERVES 6

To marinate the wings, in a large mixing bowl combine all of the marinade ingredients, stirring well.

Place the chicken in a shallow baking pan and cover with the marinade. Seal the pan with plastic wrap and let marinate for a minimum of 6 hours, preferably overnight.

To cook the wings, remove them from the marinade and reserve a small amount for basting the wings during cooking. Grill according to the method described on page 19, making sure to baste the wings continually.

Serve with chilled Chipotle Ranch Dipping Sauce.

GARLIC MARINADE

2 cups vermouth (or dry white wine)

1 cup soy sauce

1 cup olive oil

6 large garlic cloves, passed through a garlic press

2 tablespoons freshly ground black pepper

30 large chicken wings, jointed and small wing joint removed

Chipotle Ranch Dipping Sauce (page 84)

Here is a simple way to create a delicious orange wing glaze that is the perfect, cirtusy accompaniment to grilled or broiled wings. It's like duck sauce, with a good, spicy kick thanks to a dash of hot sauce and a dollop of chili sauce. Try this excellent glaze on grilled Long Island duck, too.

SERVES 6

In a medium-size saucepan over medium heat, combine the water and sugar; simmer until reduced by half, about 12 minutes. Stir in the orange juice and add the rest of the ingredients except the wings. Simmer until the mixture is about the consistency of thin maple syrup, another 10 minutes. Let the glaze cool before you baste it on your wings.

Barbecue the wings over indirect heat in a 350 degree grill, lid down (see method described on page 19). Apply a light coating of the glaze immediately after taking the wings off the grill, when they are piping hot. Alternatively, broil the wings on an ungreased baking sheet in a single layer according to the method described on page 21, applying an even coating of the glaze after removing them from the oven.

1 cup water
1 cup granulated sugar
Juice of 4 large oranges
1/4 cup prepared chili sauce (such as Heinz)
2 tablespoons honey
2 tablespoons lime juice
1 teaspoon hot sauce

30 chicken wings, jointed and small wing joint removed.

CLASSIC ORANGE GLAZED WINGS

BBQ PIT
WINGS

Since caveman times, every man worth his salt could roast meat over the fire and technically call it barbecue. What separates the good barbecuers from the great ones is patience . . . and a good sauce. The patience part is easy. Get a good, slow fire going and cook your wings covered over indirect heat, letting the barbecue work its smoky magic. The sauce part is harder to master. No matter how great your sauce is, you always wonder if a pinch more of this, or a dash more of that will improve your "secret" recipe. The fun, of course, is in the endless experimenting you can do with barbecue sauces and glazes. You have to try pretty hard to mess one up, but I encourage you to use the following recipes as a template—and try anyway!

While I am usually content to grab a bottle of Open Pit at my local supermarket when planning a chicken barbecue, I was surprised to learn how simple—and fun —making your own barbecue sauce can be. Obviously, the variations are limited only by your imagination and the contents of your spice rack. Here is a simple "base" recipe that can serve as a starting point for creating your own wing barbecue sauces (and this recipe is perfect for ribs, brisket, and whole chicken as well). This sauce is also great, served warm, as a dipping sauce for deep-frled wings (and excellent for larger chicken parts, brisket, and ribs, for that matter)!

SERVES 6

In a medium-size saucepan over medium heat, warm the oil. Then add the onion and garlic and cook slowly, until soft. Add the ketchup, vinegar, Worcestershire sauce, brown sugar, chili powder, cayenne pepper, and cumin. Raise the heat and let the sauce simmer, stirring often. Simmer until the sauce is thick enough to stick—literally—to your ribs, about 10 minutes. Add the hot pepper sauce, if desired.

Barbecue the wings over indirect heat in a 350 degree barbecue, lid down, following the method described on page 19. Apply a light coating of the sauce during the last 5 minutes of cooking. Serve the wings with the remaining sauce on the side. Alternatively, deep-fry or bake the wings according to the method described on page 20 and serve with the sauce, warm, on the side for dipping.

1/4 cup vegetable oil
1 onion, finely chopped
6 large garlic cloves, finely chopped
1 1/2 cups ketchup
1/2 cup cider vinegar
1/3 cup Worcestershire sauce
1/3 cup packed brown sugar
2 teaspoons chili powder
1/2 teaspoon cayenne pepper
1/2 teaspoon cumin
Hot pepper sauce, to taste
 (optional)

30 chicken wings

The first and most important step in making authentic Texas-style barbecue is a great "mop." The mop, so called because it is usually applied with the household apparatus of the same name, is basically a marinade, basting sauce, and dipping sauce all in one. Real Texas barbecue masters mop several dozen chickens, slabs of ribs, and briskets at a time, so they need an actual string mop to handle the task.

SERVES 4 (WITH BARBECUE SAUCE LEFT OVER)

In a large sauté pan on a medium-high flame, add the olive oil and butter. Add the onion, garlic, and shallots, and sauté until transparent, about 5 minutes. Add the tomatoe purée, tomato paste, 1/2 cup beer, the water, vinegar, and Worcestershire sauce and heat until simmering, about 5 minutes. Lower the heat to medium and add the brown sugar, chili powder, mustard powder, cumin, and cayenne; simmer for 30 minutes.

Remove the barbecue sauce from heat, pour into a bowl, and cover, reserving 1 cup of the sauce in a separate medium-size bowl. Add 1 cup of beer to the reserved 1 cup of sauce to make a barbecue mop; mix thoroughly.

Grill the wings according to the method described on page 19, basting the wings periodically with the barbecue mop. During the last 10 minutes of cooking (with the lid closed), baste the wings with the full-strength barbecue sauce.

Serve the wings hot off the grill with the remaining barbecue sauce on the side.

MARINADE AND DIPPING SAUCE

2 tablespoons olive oil
1/2 cup (1 stick) unsalted butter
1 white onion, finely chopped
5 large garlic cloves, passed
   through a garlic press
3 shallots, finely chopped
1 1/2 cups canned tomato purée
1/2 cup tomato paste
1 1/2 cups beer
1/2 cup water
3 tablespoons vinegar
2 tablespoons Worcestershire
   sauce
3 tablespoons brown sugar
1 tablespoon chili powder
1 teaspoon mustard powder
1 teaspoon dried cumin
1/2 teaspoon cayenne pepper

30 chicken wings, small wing joint
   removed

TEXAS-STYLE WINGS

It is generally agreed that deep-frying imparts the most flavor and produces the moistest wings. Fat equals flavor, and—at roughly 1,500 calories per six-wing serving—you are getting lots of both. That being said, I strongly encourage you to cast aside your modern-day hesitations and embrace these fat-filled, delicious wings with every ounce of your soul. You can hit the treadmill tomorrow.

SERVES 8

To marinate the chicken, in a large nonreactive bowl, combine the beer, soy sauce, olive oil, white wine vinegar, water, and garlic. Add the chicken wings, cover, and let marinate, refrigerated, for at least 1 hour and at most overnight.

To prepare the batter, sift the flour into a large bowl. Add the salt and pepper, eggs, oil, and 1/4 cup of the water. Stir with a whisk, gradually adding the remaining water until the flour is completely incorporated.

Heat a medium-size saucepan over medium heat, and add the oil, letting it warm in the pan. Add the onion and garlic and cook slowly until soft and golden brown, about 10 minutes. Add the vinegar, Worcestershire sauce, ketchup, brown sugar, and spices. Raise the heat until simmering. Stir often, simmering until the flavors are seamlessly blended and the sauce is thick enough to stick to the wings. Adjust the heat level of the sauce with hot sauce if desired. Set aside in a covered nonreactive bowl.

MARINADE
1 cup beer
1/4 cup soy sauce
1/2 cup olive oil
1/2 cup white wine vinegar
1 cup warm water
5 large garlic cloves, pressed

BATTER
1 1/2 cups flour
1 teaspoon salt
1 teaspoon freshly ground black
   pepper
2 large eggs
3 teaspoons peanut oil
1/2 cup water

BBQ DIPPING SAUCE
1/4 cup vegetable oil
1 onion, finely chopped
6 large garlic cloves, finely chopped
1/2 cup cider vinegar
1/3 cup Worcestershire sauce

(CONTINUES)

Coat the wings individually in the batter, and place them on a wire rack to allow the excess batter to drip off (for about 5 minutes). Once the batter is "set," carefully lower each wing into the hot oil, and deep-fry for 12 to 15 minutes, until the batter is uniformly crisp (see method for Deep-Frying Wings in a Fryer, page 16). Set aside to drain on paper towels.

Serve the wings hot from the fryer (or frying pan) with the warm barbecue dipping sauce on the side.

BBQ DIPPING SAUCE (CONTINUED)

1 1/2 cups ketchup

1/3 cup brown sugar

2 teaspoons chili powder

1/2 teaspoon cayenne pepper

1/2 teaspoon ground cumin

Hot sauce to taste (optional)

40 chicken wings, small wing joint removed

Oil for deep-frying

DEEP-FRIED WINGS

WITH SMOKY SWEET BARBECUE SAUCE

Here is an easy way to get the flavor of a deliciously smoky barbecue sauce without having to break out the grill. The juxtaposition of crispy fried chicken batter and sweet, sticky barbecue sauce give these wings a lot of flavor and a great variety of textures. I like to slather the warm barbecue sauce over the wings and break out extra napkins for my guests, but you can also serve these wings with the sauce on the side as a dip.

SERVES 6

in a large saucepan over high heat, mix together the Smoky Barbecue Sauce ingredients, stirring frequently. Bring the mixture to a rapid simmer, then reduce the heat to low. Simmer for 25 minutes, or until the sauce is reduced by half. Remove from the heat, and cover to keep warm.

To batter the wings, set out 2 small bowls. In one, mix together the flour, salt, and pepper. In the other, beat the egg with the milk. Lightly dredge each wing in the flour mixture, then in the egg mixture, and finally in the flour mixture again. The wings should have a uniform coating of batter.

Once all the wings are coated, deep-fry them using the method described on page 16. Drain on paper towels. Brush on a generous coating of the warm Smoky Barbecue Sauce and serve immediately. Alternatively, serve the deep-fried wings with the warm sauce on the side.

SMOKY BARBECUE SAUCE

2$\frac{1}{2}$ cups ketchup

1 cup white wine vinegar

$\frac{1}{2}$ cup honey

$\frac{1}{2}$ cup unsulphured molasses

2 teaspoons liquid smoke

1 teaspoon salt

$\frac{1}{2}$ teaspoon onion powder

$\frac{1}{2}$ teaspoon mild chili powder

$\frac{1}{2}$ teaspoon ground cumin

BATTER

2 cups all-purpose flour

3 teaspoons salt

1 teaspoon freshly ground black pepper

1 egg

1 cup whole milk

40 chicken wings, small wing joint removed

Oil for deep-frying

Not all barbecue sauce is the red, tomato-based stuff that most of us are familiar with. In fact, in eastern North Carolina, barbecue sauce is spicy and vinegar based. Traditionally used for sliced and "pulled" pork, this sauce is equally good as a chicken marinade—and incredible as a dipping sauce.

SERVES 6

Mix all the ingredients except the wings well. Let the sauce stand for at least 3 hours. That's it! (Most folks from eastern N.C. recommend letting this mixture sit for as long as possible, and many keep this sauce bottled for weeks at a time, claiming that it only improves the flavor.)

Grill the chicken according to the method described on page 19, being careful not to singe the wing tips. Apply a light coating of the sauce during the final 10 minutes of grilling and baste frequently to keep the wings moist. Serve the wings hot, with cold beer and room-temperature sauce on the side.

1 cup cider vinegar
2 tablespoons salt
1/2 teaspoon freshly ground black pepper
1/4 teaspoon cayenne pepper
1 teaspoon dried red pepper flakes
1 tablespoon brown sugar

30 chicken wings

Just about every region of the southern United States can claim its own type of barbecue style. The mustard-based barbecue sauce or "dressing" herein originated in the deeper South, specifically South Carolina and Georgia, where it's typically used as a basting and serving sauce for sliced pork and brisket. I happen to like it on my wings as a dipping sauce, as an alternative to blue cheese dressing or classic tomato-based barbecue sauces.

SERVES 6

In a medium-size saucepan over medium heat, melt the butter (to prevent the other ingredients from sticking). Gradually add the rest of the ingredients except the wings to the pan, stirring until smooth. Let the mixture come to a simmer, then lower heat. Simmer for approximately 20 minutes, and set aside to cool. This sauce can be refrigerated (if bottled or well covered) for up to 2 weeks.

Slowly barbecue the wings in a covered grill over medium indirect heat for approximately 35 minutes (see page 19 for details), then serve with the mustard sauce on the side for dipping.

2 tablespoons unsalted butter
1 cup yellow mustard
$\frac{1}{2}$ cup red wine vinegar
$\frac{1}{2}$ cup white wine vinegar
$\frac{1}{2}$ cup granulated sugar
2 teaspoons salt
1 tablespoon Worcestershire sauce
$1\frac{1}{2}$ teaspoons freshly ground black pepper
Tabasco sauce to taste (optional)

30 chicken wings, jointed and small wing tip removed

For me, milling around the grill with my friends, ice-cold beer and tongs in hand, is what casual entertaining is all about. If you are having some friends over for steaks or fish on the grill, why not grill up a batch of wings as well? This traditional honey barbecue sauce makes a great wing glaze—and doubles as a dipping sauce on the side. You should always marinate chicken before putting it on the grill—the spices not only add flavor to the meat, but the acidity in the garlic, onions, vinegar, and fruit juice helps to gently tenderize it. Remember to marinate for at least 12 hours, if possible, for the best results.

SERVES 6

To make the barbecue glaze, combine the tomato paste, water, honey, vinegar, chile, garlic, salt, and pepper. Bring the mixture to a boil. Reduce heat, and simmer the sauce on a low flame for approximately 15 minutes, or until the chile is tender. Transfer the sauce to a blender or food processor and blend until smooth. Set aside.

Grill the chicken according to the method discussed on page 19, being careful not to singe the wing tips. Apply the glaze, reserving half for the dipping sauce, during the final 10 minutes of grilling. Serve hot, with cold beer and the reserved barbecue dipping sauce on the side.

HONEY BARBECUE GLAZE
AND DIPPING SAUCE

1 tablespoon tomato paste

$1/2$ cup water

$1/4$ cup honey

$1/4$ cup cider vinegar

1 dried ancho chile, stemmed and seeded

1 garlic clove, crushed

Salt and freshly ground black pepper

30 chicken wings, small wing joint removed

Glazes are thick, usually semisweet sauces that can be applied immediately before or after cooking. When you apply it after cooking, the heat of the meat serves to cook the glaze in, and gives your dish a lovely shiny, glazed appearance and a nice color. The simplest glazes can be reductions of sweet juices. For example, boiling down a quart of apple cider until syrupy produces a wonderfully sweet apple glaze that is perfect for pork ribs or a whole roast. Here is a great all-purpose glaze for wings. You can also use this glaze recipe on whole chicken, roasted meats, and ribs.

SERVES 6

In a medium-size saucepan over medium heat, warm the olive oil. Add the garlic, sautéing it until it is lightly gold. Add the whiskey, ketchup, vinegar, and Worcestershire sauce and blend well. Continue stirring and add the brown sugar gradually. Add the mustard powder next, and continue to stir until the mixture simmers and the brown sugar is fully dissolved. Stir in the lemon juice, salt, and pepper. Remove from heat and let cool to room temperature. Store the mixture, covered, in the refrigerator until ready to use.

Prepare a medium fire on your grill, and cook the wings over indirect heat according to the method described on page 19, basting the wings with a light coating of glaze during the last 10 minutes of cooking. The glaze can be served on the side as a dipping sauce.

ALL-PURPOSE GLAZE

1 tablespoon olive oil

3 garlic cloves, finely minced (or passed through a garlic press)

$1/2$ cup bourbon whiskey (or dark rum if preferred)

$1/2$ cup ketchup

$1/3$ cup white wine vinegar

1 teaspoon Worcestershire sauce

$1/4$ cup packed brown sugar

$1/4$ teaspoon mustard powder

$1/2$ tablespoon freshly squeezed lemon juice

Salt and freshly ground black pepper to taste

30 chicken wings, jointed and small wing joint removed

BBQ WINGS WITH ALL-PURPOSE GLAZE

WING
DIPPING
SAUCES

I used to make fun of my college friend Joe for always eating an ungodly amount of ketchup with his french fries. Such was his love of the condiment that Joe was wont to explain, "My friend, the fry is merely a vehicle for the ketchup." To me, that describes perfectly a good wing dipping sauce. If you, like me, continually challenge yourself to see just how much blue cheese dressing you can transfer from the bowl to your mouth, via a wing, at the local pub, then you'll enjoy trying these recipes. After all, sometimes the dip is the best part!

CHIPOTLE RANCH DIPPING SAUCE

Here's a refreshing departure from the traditional blue cheese wing dip that uses cool ranch dressing with a spicy pepper kick. Try to locate chipotle peppers in your local grocery or gourmet shop. If you can't, you can substitute pickled red or green peppers without changing the recipe too dramatically.

YIELDS APPROXIMATELY 3 CUPS

Peel the cucumbers, slice them in half lengthwise, and remove the seeds. Add the cucumbers and chipotle to a blender or food processor and purée until somewhat smooth.

Transfer to a medium bowl and add the mayonnaise, buttermilk, scallions, parsley, celery seed, garlic powder, onion powder, paprika, cayenne pepper, salt, and pepper. Refrigerate for at least 2 to 3 hours.

2 medium cucumbers

1 canned chipotle chile, seeded

1 cup mayonnaise

1 cup buttermilk (or whole milk if necessary)

2 tablespoons chopped scallions, green part only

2 teaspoons minced parsley

2 teaspoons celery seed

$\frac{1}{4}$ teaspoon garlic powder

$\frac{1}{4}$ teaspoon onion powder

$\frac{1}{4}$ teaspoon paprika

$\frac{1}{8}$ teaspoon cayenne pepper

$\frac{1}{4}$ teaspoon salt

$\frac{1}{4}$ teaspoon black pepper

Perhaps the most popular chile pepper in the world, the jalapeño is a natural for wing sauces. As hot as these stubby green chile peppers may seem, among the hardcore chile pepper fanatics they hardly even rate on the heat scale—rating a "meager" 2,500 to 5,000 Scoville heat units, compared to upwards of 200,000 for habanero peppers! When dried and smoked, jalapeños become chipotle peppers—another spicy but not too intense ingredient often used in salsas. Here's a simple honey mustard dressing with a spicy jalapeño kick that goes great with any kind of wings.

YIELDS ABOUT ¾ CUP

In a small saucepan, heat the vinegar. Once warm, add the mustard, honey, and jalapeño. Boil for 2 minutes. Remove from the heat and serve.

½ cup red wine vinegar
2 tablespoons mustard
1 tablespoon honey
1 jalapeño pepper, halved lengthwise

JALAPEÑO DIPPING SAUCE

There is something about the combination of sweet and spicy flavors that goes great with chicken wings, and this easy-to-prepare honey-mustard sauce (with a dash of hot pepper) fills the bill. I like to use chunky German-style mustard, which has lots of whole brown and yellow mustard seeds, to contrast with the smooth and creamy texture of the dip, but you can use whatever mustard you prefer.

YIELDS ABOUT 1½ CUPS

In a small bowl, combine the mayonnaise, mustard, and honey, and whisk until thoroughly combined. Add the onion, hot sauce, Worcestershire sauce, and celery seed, and whisk until blended. Chill in the refrigerator for 1 hour prior to serving.

1 cup mayonnaise

⅓ cup prepared German-style mustard

¼ cup honey

½ small onion, finely grated

½ tablespoon hot pepper sauce

1 tablespoon Worcestershire sauce

¼ teaspoon celery seed

If there's anything I like better than regular blue cheese sauce on my wings, it's Roquefort dressing. A goat's-milk cheese aged in the limestone caverns of Mount Combalou, near the village of Roquefort in southwestern France, Roquefort is generally more comfortable next to a bottle of first-growth Bordeaux than a plate of steaming deep-fried chicken wings. However, this particular sauce is so addictive that it takes a Herculean effort to prevent yourself from rudely licking the sauce bowl clean after the wings are gone.

YIELDS ABOUT 3 CUPS

In a medium bowl, cream together the butter and cheese, using a plastic spatula, until smooth. Set aside.

In a medium saucepan over high heat, boil the vermouth and green peppercorns until the liquid is reduced to half, about 15 minutes. Lower the heat to medium, add the cream, and cook the mixture until it is reduced by half, about 15 minutes. Reduce the heat to low, and gradually add the cheese mixture, stirring with a whisk. Add the parsley, grind pepper into the sauce to taste, and serve warm.

1 cup unsalted butter, at room temperature
2 cups imported Roquefort, at room temperature
2 cups dry vermouth
5 teaspoons green peppercorns
2 cups heavy cream
2 tablespoons chopped fresh parsley

This sweet Thai chile sauce is traditionally served alongside roasted or barbecued meats, and happens to perfectly complement grilled chicken wings. If you cannot find Thai chile peppers (thin, tiny, carrot-shaped peppers available in red, orange, and green varieties), you may substitute several jalapeños or Scotch bonnets.

YIELDS ABOUT 2 CUPS

In a small saucepan, combine all of the ingredients and bring them to a boil. Reduce heat to very low, cover, and simmer for 45 minutes to 1 hour, or until the sauce is thickened. Taste and adjust the seasonings as necessary. Transfer to small dipping dishes.

8 Thai red chile peppers, seeded (see page 51)
4 garlic cloves, crushed in a garlic press
1 shallot, minced
1 28-ounce can whole tomatoes
$2/3$ cup granulated sugar
$2/3$ cup rice vinegar
2 teaspoons salt

When you are in the mood for classic wings but not the intense flavor of blue cheese dressing, try making a simple lemon mayonnaise instead. It is the perfect accompaniment to baked or deep-fried wings—and also makes a pretty good sandwich spread or dip for fresh vegetables! For more flavor, try spicing up this simple recipe with sliced scallions, mustard, capers, or even anchovies.

YIELDS 1 CUP

1 cup mayonnaise

1 tablespoon finely grated lemon zest

1 tablespoon fresh lemon juice

2 teaspoons coarse-grain or regular Dijon mustard

Pinch of salt

Pinch of freshly ground black pepper

In a small bowl, whisk together the mayonnaise, lemon zest, lemon juice, mustard, salt, and pepper until well combined.

The best part of eating Chicken McNuggets (and I think we can all admit that we enjoy them) is invariably the dipping sauce. I happen to like the sweet-and-sour variety, but, on the whole, I find the flavor as overly processed as the chicken itself. A great (and probably much healthier) alternative to McNuggets are wings with this delicious homemade sweet-and-sour dipping sauce, which is quite simple to prepare.

YIELDS 1 1/2 CUPS

Combine the cornstarch and ¼ cup of the pineapple juice; reserve. In a saucepan, combine the remaining ¾ cup of pineapple juice, ketchup, red wine vinegar, soy sauce, brown sugar, ginger, salt, and pepper. Bring to a simmer over medium heat. Add the cornstarch mixture and reduce heat to low. Continue to simmer until the sauce thickens, about 12 minutes. Let cool, and serve as a dipping sauce for baked, fried, or grilled wings.

You may also use this sauce as a glaze for grilled wings, brushing it on during the last 2 minutes of cooking or immediately after they come off the hot grill.

½ tablespoon cornstarch
1 cup pineapple juice, divided
½ cup ketchup
⅓ teaspoon red wine vinegar
1 teaspoon soy sauce
½ tablespoon brown sugar
½ teaspoon minced fresh ginger
Pinch of salt
Pinch of black pepper

This is a classic Asian dipping sauce, velvety smooth and rich in peanut flavor. Thai "fish sauce" can usually be found in the local supermarket's ethnic foods aisle, sometimes under the name "seasoning sauce."

YIELDS ABOUT 1 CUP

To make the peanut sauce, add the peanuts along with the peanut oil to a food processor. Blend, on high, until the peanuts form a rough paste. Add the rest of the ingredients except for the cilantro; blend until smooth. Stir in the cilantro and thin with peanut oil to taste.

$1/2$ cup unsalted roasted peanuts
1 tablespoon peanut oil, plus more to taste
2 fresh Thai chiles or other small chiles
1 $1/2$-inch-thick slice fresh ginger
4 garlic cloves
$1/3$ cup canned unsweetened coconut milk
2 teaspoons low-sodium soy sauce
4 teaspoons fish sauce
1 teaspoon granulated sugar
1 tablespoon fresh lime juice
Pinch of salt (add to taste, as fish sauce can be very salty)
$1/2$ cup finely minced cilantro leaves and stems

THAI PEANUT SAUCE

Chicken Wings Are Not for Flying

ferryhalim.com/original/gl/chicken.htm

This site has a great wing-themed game for online fun—help to save the "stubborn little chickens" from hitting the ground by throwing them umbrellas to help cushion their descent.

BuffaloWings.com

www.buffalowings.com

The Bellissimos lay their claim to—and try to make a buck off of—wing history on the aptly named "buffalowings.com," the official site of Buffalo, New York's Anchor Bar and birthplace of the wing of the same name. Sandwiched in between the usual advertising hyperbole and promotional copy are amusing "wing facts" and a complete historical account of the Buffalo wing's invention by the inventor herself. Plus, the Anchor Bar will "send wings just about any-where" if you have a burning desire to taste the original recipe that started it all.

Peggy Trowbridge's "Home Cooking" on About.com

homecooking.about.com/library/

weekly/aa042301b.htm

The host of About.com's Home Cooking section really lays out the whole history of chicken wings, including health facts (surprise—they are fatten-ing), dozens of great recipes, and general prepa-ration tips.

Fabulous Food's Wing Preparation Guide

www.fabulousfoods.com/school/cstech/

chixwings.html

The "Cooking School" portion of Cheri Sicard's wonderful site features a pictorial display of preparing chicken wings for appetizers and demystifies the different joints of the wing. Cheri thoughtfully includes a link to her "stocks" page, which can help you figure out how to use all of those discarded wing tips.

Stuffed Thai Chicken Wings

www.atasteofthai.com/app13.htm

I wish I developed this recipe—basically wings stuffed with pork and spices and served with a tomato-basil curry sauce. I found this site on the back of a can of coconut milk and was pleasantly surprised to find the excellent wing recipe. The company sells several products that are great for making Thai sauces, including powdered red curry base, canned coconut milk, and prepared peanut sauce mix that's great in a pinch. Want to try the Indian version? See the recipe by Chef Sanjeev Kapoor (www.sanjeevkapoor.com/recipes/thaicuisine/stufchicwings.html).

Chicken Wings—The Movie

www.7mpictures.com/inside/wings.htm

If you thought you loved wings, this minute-long short film will convince you that there are others who love them more than you do. Watch in awe as a rather large man in a Hawaiian shirt makes short work of about a dozen Buffalo wings. The film was produced by 7M pictures, a company whose mission statement includes producing "quality entertainment of commercial value and artistic integrity."

I collect small pleasures like some people collect playing cards off the street—eventually trying to put together an entire deck. This is my fifth book on small pleasures, after writing about Bloody Mary cocktails, ribs, chili, and hot toddies. Thanks again to Chris Pavone, who gave me the first card in my deck, and to the entire editorial team of Clarkson Potter, who provided the inspiration for this latest one. Adina Steiman, my editor, must also be thanked, both for fueling my penchant for writing about alcoholic beverages and foods rich in trans-fatty acids—and for taking me out to indulge in them occasionally. My gratitude also goes out to Jane Treuhaft for another eye-catching design, and to Susan Westendorf and Felix Gregorio for skillfully ferrying the book through the production process. Thanks to Willie Nash, the photographer of all of my books (and also one of my best friends), for his advice, friendship, and flexibility. Working with Liza Jernow, our food stylist, Willie has published his best food photography yet.

ACKNOWLEDGMENTS

INDEX

Born and raised in New York City, Chris has tempered his lifelong fascination with foods heavy in saturated fats and alcoholic beverages with a successful career in media. Since graduating Connecticut College in 1990, Chris has been a magazine editor, writer, marketer, new media producer, and advertising executive. The author of *The Bloody Mary, Ribs, The Ultimate Chili Book,* and *Hot Toddies,* Chris and his books have been featured on the Food Network's "Cooking Today," NBC's "Today Show," CBS's "Early Show," and periodicals including the *New York Post, Boston Herald,* the *Miami Herald,* and *Glamour* and *Playboy* magazines.

CRUNCHYBAKEDATOMICFRIEDGA